THE DANCING BEARS

BY W. S. MERWIN

New Haven

Yale University Press

1954

Copyright, 1954, by Yale University Press.
Printed in the United States of America by the
Printing-Office of the Yale University Press.
All rights reserved. This book may not be
reproduced, in whole or in part, in any form
(except by reviewers for the public press),
without written permission from the publishers.
ACKNOWLEDGMENTS: *These poems have appeared*
in THE HUDSON REVIEW, KENYON REVIEW, POETRY,
FURIOSO, HARPER'S, BOTTEGHE OSCURE *in the*
United States; THE LISTENER, MANDRAKE, THE POET,
NEW POEMS 1953 *in England.* "*East of the Sun*
and West of the Moon," "*Fable,*" *and the three*
Cansos have been read on the BBC Third Programme.

Library of Congress catalog card number: 54-5087.

FOR DIDO

—marveling

CONTENTS

TOWER

Now I have come again
To the common country
Where all faces are mirrors and tell me
I return white-faced as the dawn.

Have I outrun belief
And walk in a superstition?
Ignorant and alone,
Without haste I went only

Among the innocent
Noon-laden fields, then
Among thickets, the way growing
Black and white and thorny,

And at the cockshut hour
—The summer dusk among
Its hedges drowsing—came
Upon the odor of apples,

Upon a darkling tower
Hung with no flutter of birds,
Puff of smoke or banner;
And when I called

No echo stirred nor answer,
Pin nor shutter, only
By the door a hanging wheel
In no wind was turning slowly.

Round and still as a finger
Laid upon lips, stone
Above stone, the tower. Its shadow
Fell as far as evening.

Dark spool wound within silence,
Ringed with stillness as with trees
—Birches stood hushed in the green air,
And moat-lapped apple trees.

Polished were the dark stones;
As ice they rose. Is it
That there the crevices
Run at neck-level always,

That where that water stands
Almost as ice, the rippling
Tails of salmon cut
The throats of all reflection?

I saw my body
As a smooth alien
On stones and water walking
Headless, not noticing;

And my head, drifting
Bereft of body, gave me
Again from every stone
My astonishment.

A pebble might have rung
A crash of seven years' portent,
On that water falling.
Or turn away the face.

But there was enough of portent
Folding that stony bobbin
If the failing light could limn
And limb such legerdemain.

And what if all motion
Were a web into that stance
And all shattering
But served that severance?

I cannot learn from mirrors
Or faces of this country
Which of me, head or body,
Still fronts itself there,

Still winds in unmoving dance
About itself while the shadows
Turn alike about flesh
About stone, about trees,

Till dizzy would the wind be
If wind there were; and yet
No apple falls, nor the green
Light like leaves from the trees;

And from somewhere unseen
The deceitful magpie sings,
"Love, love, oh lover,
Oh King live forever."

RUNES FOR A

ROUND TABLE

Capricorn

Where darkness is
Once a mirror was
And I therein was king.
Bearded, lecherous,
Still I stand recalling
The windy cities
Like reeds wailing.

Aquarius

This is faithbearing:
All seas turning
On one's shoulders, to stand
Patiently as though painted
Though the fish be gone.

Pisces

Let the stars quaver
In night blue as a pool;
I rise, though the tide fall,
I turn, but I am still
And wiser than any water
In the eddying sky.

Aries

I bear suspicion
Like a golden fleece,
And horns like auguries
Curling into nothing;
On these the world has wheeled.

Taurus

White as a flower,
As a floating flower,
As a white child,
Eleven kings I wield;
Afloat in gentle water,
I trample on what is,
I am what is to be.

Gemini

He sinks when I rise,
He laughs when I die;
We twain are single
As the same rain falling
On two sides of a tree.

Cancer

Multitudes bow to me
On shores where no wave bows,
To me who slip sideways
In the heat of the day
With the blank stars for sand.

Leo

What greater ravage
Than this: to become
The multiple shield
Of the gilt marauder,
To hold a honeycomb,
Whose taste was for rage.

Virgo

Not so much as a song
In my most silver dream
Has ravished my ear.
Damage by beast and man
And by the scandalous sun
Sing out, but I am not there.

Libra

One man confronting two,
Each side on twelve legs walking,
Yet is no balance between:
The one outweighs the two,
For all hands are uneven
But the wheel is equal.

Scorpio

All unbidden
I offer an island;
Let the bidden man
Turn, flee like a season;
Mine is the turning end;
My bitterness, immortal,
Finds the mortal heel.

Sagittarius

All quarry flees. The arrow
Drawn always to my ear I still
Have not let fly, and yet they fall.

THE LADY WITH

THE HERON

I walk athirst
In a month of rain;
Drought I learned
At the feet of a heron.

Green trees, full rivers;
Athirst I went,
With a shrieking bird
In the drawn breath.

At the only spring
When I went for water
I met a lady
And thirst I had none.

I say, at the fountain
There I met a lady,
She led a blue heron
By the beck of her hand.

Moon-wise the owl is,
The wren not tame,
But I unlearned patience
At the feet of a heron.

So deep a water
As those her eyes
Kissed I never
At the lip of April.

Drink, sir, she said,
Of so sweet water.
The bird was blind
That she led by a shadow.

Lady, I said,
Thirst is no longer.
But she led my eyes
By the beck of her hand.

Of her eyes I drank
And no other water.
Hope I unlearned
At the feet of a bird,

And saw no face
When I bent there;
Such saw I never
In other water.

My lips not wet,
Yet was she gone
Leading a heron
By the shade of her hand.

And my eyes thirst
On the birdless air;
Blindness I learned
At the feet of a heron.

WHEN I CAME

FROM COLCHIS

When I came from Colchis
Where the spring fields lay green,
A land famed for fine linen,
Bounded northerly
By the glistering Caucasus,
By the Euxine westerly,

Most I spoke of fine linen
But did, in truth, tell something
Of Jason who had come sailing
And poised upon that shore
His fabulous excursion.
All turned the incredulous ear.

From Troy, over the water
Returning, I recounted
The tale of wrecked walls, but said
That gray waves lap and surround
That shore as any other.
With a shrewd smile they listened.

Now if, amazed, I come
From the deep bourn of your hand,
A stranger up from the sunned
Sea of your eyes, lady,
What fable should I tell them,
That they should believe me?

You, Genoese mariner,
Your face most perfectly
A mask about a vision,
Your eyes most clear when turned
On the bewildering west,
You, so your story goes,
Who believed that that direction
Toward which all breath and knowledge
Although their eyes cling elsewhere
Make ignorant declension,
Must by its own token,
Continuing, contain
A grammar of return,
A world's unknown dimension,
You, nevertheless, in search
Of gilt and spice, who fancied
Earth too circumscribed
To imagine and cradle,
Where no map had suspected,
The distances and marvels,
The unfingered world—
I whose face has become,
Oh mistaken sailor,
Suddenly a frame
For astonishment, stand
In the long light of wonder

Staring upon the shadows
That circle and return
From another's eyes,
I, after so long,
Who have been wrong as you.

FABLE

I am a mad precarious man
Making a prayer for folly
At the midnight and heartless hour,
Moon-beset, and my best of prayer
Is incontinently to complain
Upon a foolish story.

Long ago in a laurel wood—
Pray for the love of folly—
Once a lover, and he heartless,
And his lady, heartless likewise,
Loving, but without heart, there stood,
And they wept grievously.

He said: As though with a heart I grieve—
Pray for the poor in folly—
That we in whom great love there is
Should love less well than loveless bodies
For scarcely do we dare to love
Lest we love heartlessly.

She said: Some stint there must be done—
Pray for the lips of folly—
For how should we this pain abide
As thorough as though hearts we had
Yet suffer and love as though alone,
However entwined we be.

So they one heart between them made—
Pray for the hands of folly—
Of all heat and belief they knew,
For the sustenance whereof they two
Made tributary their own blood
And rejoiced heartily.

Dark it was in the laurel wood—
Pray for the eyes of folly—
A noise as of a breathing beast
Swung between them; when they kissed,
All about them it raged and played,
But nothing could they see.

Reverence overcame them then—
Pray for the heart of folly—
That they out of mere need could make
From nothing and a bit of dark
What had failed them from their creation,
And they sank upon knee.

And most religiously they swore—
Pray for the word of folly—
That never would they look upon
The warm marvel that beat between,
Lest, should their eyes prove so familiar,
It take offense and die.

So they took heart, and the heart, grown wild—
Pray for the limbs of folly—
Would lunge on the hollow dark like pain,
And then, till love came round again,
Lie and be gentled like a child
And feed on intimacy.

Almost nine hours they lived at ease—
Pray for the life of folly—
Yet dawn, ubiquitous, could watch
How they grew curious till each,
Unknown to the other, raised his eyes
Out of their dark and pity

And saw within the other's eyes—
Pray for the bells of folly—
Where they all tenderness had set,
Burning upon the day, a great
Bull-shouldered beast with horns of brass
Who cried in fury,

Who lunged between them like all pain—
Pray for the death of folly—
In mortal rage, till brass and beast
Gored nothing but the ground at last,
And empty, where a heart had been,
Love's body lay.

Ghosts are heartless that tease the blood—
Pray for the soul of folly—
And ghostly as a coil of rain
Heartless they stood once again,
Day-stricken in the laurel wood,
And they wept grievously.

I am a sullen unseemly man—
Pray now no more for folly—
Who in the bleak and tolling hour
Walk like a chime without a tower,
Rending a story, and complain
Heartless and foolishly.

THE PASSION

In that garden at evening
We could not speak save in prayer
Unto each other saying,
"Each other's will be done";
Nor could we walk under
Bare thorn but the branches
Unnaturally would compose
Over our heads a crown.
  Non enim sciunt quid faciunt

Truly, strong bulls of Bashan
Had beset us round;
Our doom, though falsely, had been
Foretold, and where we came
Hands were washed of our end;
And there was that fretful spouse
Had suffered because of us,
Many things in a dream.
  Non enim sciunt quid faciunt

Each of us, we knew,
Must be unto the other
The singular cross; yet how
Could either of us hang painful
Upon the other, either
Upon the other weigh
As burden? Merrily
We went out to that hill.
Non enim sciunt quid faciunt

We heard the nails scream
In the wood as they were drawn
Out from the last time,
And felt their pain; the cry
You swore was old affection
And smiled upon the sound
Not woodenly, but I turned
My wooden face away.
Non enim sciunt quid faciunt

Three hours we hung as though
To veil the sun; thereafter
The earth shook; and, although
You said it was not real,
The dark was ours: no other
Voices, at last no thirst;
Doubt not, love, though the first
Death is original.
Non enim sciunt quid faciunt

On the stroke of our absence,
They say, the sainted dead
Rose from their double patience
In jealousy, for we seemed
Our own heaven. Through the rifted
Temple veil we saw only
Darkness, and virgins darkly
Coming with lamps untrimmed.
Non enim sciunt quid faciunt

They led us away
To this place we were to harrow
And rise from, the third day,
And howso scripture be truthful,
Yet this pain we pass through,
Though shared, consumes us by
Dividing infinitely,
Is at all times eternal.
Non enim sciunt quid faciunt

MARGERY'S SONG

I am a jill-whisper
And a cold sister
And a windy daughter
With hawthorn in my hair.

Five fingers of thin willow
Flicker my preferment;
I go feat but draughty
With a ghost of rag about me.

A nimble bird I saw:
Ruses were its children;
And friendly was the wind
But spoke me hungerly.

A little coin, a morsel,
Give me for my sleeking
For fear trespass should busy
Hands no better than bony.

Whose dish is cold and clever?
I saw a bone shiver.
In name of shadows bleating
Yet meatily the mouth feeds.

Soul is thin confusion.
I am vagary
Snared in a bony body
With hawthorn in my hair.

SONG OF THE

MAD MENAGERIE

I on whom the wild sun
Upon unvaried journey
Burned with jealousy
Because of my unreason,

Know I was legendary.
On straw I lie down.
Wise hand, be wary:
My rage is uneven.

In a cautious country
The wild shadows came down
As though athirst, came softly
And drank of the clear moon.

But the wind was tamed away,
But all the palms fell down.
The bright aviary
Sings, "O daughters of Zion."

Thirst is yet necessary:
The lean shade comes down
Of my own savagery
To sip my dry distraction.

Hands, befriend cautiously:
Now I pace alone
That mad menagerie,
The body behind bone.

SONG OF MARVELS

The day is down.
All a shiver of gold,
Age talks in the trees.
All faces rise out of the sea.

Think, think of the marvel:
One time there was a beggar
Loved a great lady
For the sake of white hands.

I hear a whisper break
Cavernous upon coral;
The hours like fishes
Wheel in amber undersea.

Sing, sing of the marvel:
A beggar with his two hands
Killed a great lady
For the love of patience.

I see the speech of leaves
That lisp in the late garden
And eyes like fishes
In deep amber waving.

Sing, sing of the marvel:
Our hands are fathomless,
Our eyes shake in the gold,
All for the love of patience.

SONG OF THREE SMILES

Let me call a ghost,
Love, so it be little:
In December we took
No thought for the weather.

Whom now shall I thank
For this wealth of water?
Your heart loves harbors
Where I am a stranger.

Where was it we lay
Needing no other
Twelve days and twelve nights
In each other's eyes?

Or was it at Babel
And the days too small
We spoke our own tongue
Needing no other?

If a seed grow green
Set a stone upon it
That it learn thereby
Holy charity.

If you must smile
Always on that other,
Cut me from ear to ear
And we all smile together.

SONG OF THE NEW FOOL

Let the sea and all her women
With their combs and white horses,
Their mirrors and shells, the green-flaming
Bushes, the bull-necked hills,

The uncombed crags, and the trees
Shading their leopards and thrushes,
The shadows and loud peacocks,
Rocks, and the laughing geese,

And the fires, and the fire that stood
Still over Jericho,
The stars and the wet moon,
And the day and the night

(But caution: for the west wind
Is secret, the west wind's hunger
All love and ghost
May not satisfy)

And laughter and the unicorn
Come in the morning
While the air is a blue girl
And eat from my hand.

For I filled my hands
With fists and cursed till the bone
Heart of the world broke;
And my hands are tender.

EAST OF THE SUN AND

WEST OF THE MOON

Say the year is the year of the phoenix.
Ordinary sun and common moon,
Turn as they may, are too mysterious
Unless such as are neither sun nor moon
Assume their masks and orbits and evolve
Neither a solar nor a lunar story
But a tale that might be human. What is a man
That a man may recognize, unless the inhuman
Sun and moon, wearing the masks of a man,
Weave before him such a tale as he
—Finding his own face in the strange story—
Mistakes by metaphor and calls his own,
Smiling, as on a familiar mystery?

The moon was thin as a poor man's daughter
At the end of autumn. A white bear came walking
On a Thursday evening at the end of autumn,
Knocked at a poor man's door in a deep wood,
And, "Charity," when the man came he said,
"And the thin hand of a girl have brought me here.
Winter will come, and the vixen wind," he said,
"And what have you but too many mouths to feed,
Oh what have you but a coat like zither-strings
To ward that fury from your family?
But I though wintry shall be bountiful

Of furs and banquets, coins like summer days,
Grant me but the hand of your youngest daughter."

"By a swooning candle, in my porchless door,
While all I wedded or sired huddle behind me,
The night unceremonious with my hair,
I know I cut a poor figure," the man said;
"And I admit that your cajolery
(For opulence was once my setting-on)
Finds me not deaf; but I must ask my daughter.
And no, she says. But come again on Thursday:
She is more beautiful than the story goes,
And a girl who wants a week for her persuading
Merits that slow extravagance," he said.
Further in autumn by a week's persuading
The youngest girl on a white bear went riding.

The moon played in a painted elder tree;
He said, when they had gone a while, "We walk
In a night so white and black, how can you tell
My shoulder from a moon-struck hill, my shadow
From the towering darkness; are you not afraid?"
And, "You are thin and colorful who ride
Alone on a white and monstrous thing; suppose
I rose up savage in a desolate place;
Are you not afraid?" And, "What if I were to wander
Down a black ladder, in a trope of death,
Through seven doors all of black ice, and come
On a land of hyperbole, stiff with extremes;
Would it not make the hair rise on your head?"

The wind with moonlit teeth rippled and sulked
In the paper trees, but three times "No," she said.
"Oh then hold fast by the hair of my shoulders,"
He said; "hold fast my hair, my savage hair;
And let your shadow as we go hold fast
The hair of my shadow, and all will be well."
Later than owls, all night, a winter night,
They traveled then, until the screaming wind
Fell behind or dead, till no stars glittered
In the headlong dark; and each step dark and long
As falling in the valley of the blind;
Yet all the while she felt her yellow hair
Hang loose at her shoulders, as though she stood still.

They came before daylight to a stone hill
Steep as a pier glass, where no shrub grew,
Nor grass rustled, nor breeze stirred before dawn.
When the bear knocked, a door swung wide. Their eyes
Enormous with the dark, a hall they entered
That blazed between mirrors, between pilasters
Of yellow chrysolite; on walls of brass
Gold branches of dead genealogies
Clutched candles and wild torches whence the flames
Rose still as brilliants. Under a fiery
Garnet tree with leaves of glass, sunken
In a pool of sea-green beryl as in still water
A gold salmon hung. And no sound came.

The wall healed behind them. When she turned,
The wall steep as a pier glass, the door
Vanished like a face in ruffled water,
And they stood dumb in the echoing light
While no flame crackled, no water fell. They passed
Between the rows of burning, between the rings
Of extinct animals that stared from sockets
In the braziered walls; hour upon hour,
Hall upon blazing hall, and came at last
Through obsequious curtains to a closed room
Where she descended; at a beck of his head
A gold table leapt from the air; she dined
That night on lapwing and wine of pomegranates

The bear had gone. She touched a silver bell.
She stood straightway in a white chamber
By a bed of lapis lazuli. Red agate
And yellow chrysolite the floors. A white
Carnelian window gave upon cut hills
Of amethyst and yellow serpentine
Pretending summer; when she stood naked there
Her nakedness from the lighted stones
Sprang a thousand times as girl or woman,
Child or staring hag. The lamps went black;
When she lay down to sleep, a young man came
Who stayed all night in the dark beside her
But was gone before dawn came to that country.

Nightly he came again. Once he said,
"I am the white bear, who once was a man;
In a christian body, in a green kingdom
One time I had dominion. Now I keep
Not so much as the shadow that I had,
And my own shape only by dark; by day
Compelled I am to that pale beast. Let it be
Ensample to your forbearance: here love
Must wander blind or with mistaken eyes,
For dissolution walks among the light
And vision is the sire of vanishing."
What love soever in the dark there were,
Always at daylight she wakened alone.

By day she walked in the espaliered garden
Among pheasants and clear flowers; she said,
"What if these pheasants amble in white glass,
Ducks strut ridiculous in stone, the streams
Slither nowhere in beryl; why should I
Complain of such inflexible content,
Presume to shudder at such serenity,
Who walk in some ancestral fantasy,
Lunar extravagance, or lost pagoda
That dreams of no discipline but indolence?
What shall be rigid but gems and details
While all dimensions dance in the same air?
And what am I if the story be not real?

But what it is," she said, "to wander in silence,
Though silence be a garden. What shall I say,
How chiseled the tongue soever, and how schooled
In sharp diphthongs and suasive rhetorics,
To the echoless air of this sufficiency?
Where should I find the sovereign aspirate
To rouse in this world a tinkle of syllables,
Or what shall I sing to crystal ears, and where
All songs drop in the air like stones; oh what
Shall I do while the white-tongued flowers shout
Impossible silence on the impossible air
But wander with my hands over my ears?
And what am I if the story be not real?

He says the place is innocent; and yet
I may not see his face; claims he is held
Equivocating between prince and beast
By the ministrations of an evil stepdame,
But such might be mere glittering deviltry.
Here is no nightly moon or tidal water
But mornings miming at mutability
Where all stands new at noon and nothing fades
Down the perfect amber of the afternoons;
All, simultaneous and unwearied, comes
Guesting again at evening. But a day
Must dwindle before dawn be real again;
And what am I if the story be not real?"

She said at night when he lay beside her,
"Why should I raise the singular dissent
Who delight in an undiminished country
Where all that was or shall be transitory
Stands whole again already? Yet I sigh
For snipes to whir and fall, for hawks to fall,
For one more mortal crimson that will fade,
For one glimpse of the twisted holly tree
Before my mother's door, and the short-lived
Wren by my mother's window, and the tame crane
Walking in shallow water. I would learn
Whether I dreamed then or walk now in a dream,
For what am I if the story be not real?"

Suddenly where no sound had been she heard
A distant lisp and crumble, like a wave,
Like the whisper of tidal water, emulous
Of its own whispers: his echoing heart. "Shall I
Pace an eternity of corridors,
Alone among sad topaz, the reflections
Flickering only on your emptiness,
And the soundlessness be like a sound of mourning,
That seemed a sound of joy? Nevertheless,
Go you shall if you wish; but promise,
Lest a malicious word undo us both,
Never to walk or talk alone," he said,
"With your mother, who is as wise as you."

It was a Sunday. Gold on the glass leaves.
She sat in the garden on the white bear's shoulders.
She touched a silver bell, and instantly
Saw the swaying of incorrigible meadows
Ripening, a green wind playful in barley,
The holly, contorted at her mother's door,
The fluttering wren—the brief feathers
Provisional about mortality—
At her mother's window, the tame crane walking
As though not real where the real shallows ran.
She had descended; the bear was gone;
She heard the whistling grass, and the holly leaves
Saying, "Your mother, who is wise as you."

She was greeted like a lost season.
Daylong she walked again in affluent summer,
But one day walked at last aside, and talked
Alone with her mother, who was wise as she.
"Equivocation between prince and beast,
The ministrations of an evil stepdame,
Might be a devilish tale; how could you tell,"
Her mother said, "should it be the devil's self
Or some marvel of ugliness you lay beside?
Take, better than advice, this end of candle
To light when he sleeps next you in the dark;
Only be careful that no drops fall."
The grass might whistle under the holly leaves.

On a day of no clouds he came to fetch her.
It was a Sunday. A soft wind stroking
The fields already white almost to harvest.
"Shall we not ride a while in the mortal air
Before we go," he asked, "for the love of fading?
But wish, when you are weary, for the sound
Of the silver bell, and we shall instantly
Be home again. Did all happen as I said?"
"Yes," she said, "how might it be otherwise?"
"Did you, then, walk aside with your mother?" he asked;
"Did you listen to your mother's advice?"
"Oh no," she said. "Then all may yet be well."
But she wished for the sound of the silver bell.

That night when she was sure he slept
She rose in the dark and struck light
To the end of candle, and held it above his face.
What blaze was this, what prince shaming with beauty
The sun peerless at noon? The dazzled stones
Seemed each a blond particular summer wringing
In the one thirst the lion and the nightingale.
The shadows bowed; they fell down amazed.
"And I with my foolish arm upraised . . .
But love so beggars me of continence,
Either I must kiss him or die," she said,
And bent, therewith, and kissed his head. Three times
The tallow folly from the candle fell.

"Oh why must all hope resolve to vanity?"
Waking, he cried; "Why could you not entertain
A curious patience but for one whole year,
For then had we been saved, and my spell broken.
Now this kingdom must shatter and I depart
For the wheeling castle of my stepmother
And marry a princess with a nose three ells long,
When I might have married you." "Oh love," she cried,
"May I not learn the way and follow you?"
"There is no way there that a body might follow:
Farther than dreams that palace lies,
East of the sun and west of the moon, girt
With rage of stars for sea. There no one comes."

She seemed to sleep, for she woke again
On a usual morning in a different world,
Bright grass blowing, birds loud in the trees;
That precious kingdom, that charmed lover
Gone. She was kneeling under a willow
In her salt tears. When she had called
And cried till she was weary she walked on
Slowly, walked the length of a day, and seemed
None the more weary for all her walking
But traveled, it seemed, in a landscape of exceptions
Where no evening came but a shadowy
Skeptical bird who settled in a tree
And sang, "All magic is but metaphor."

Under a crag, when it should have been evening,
Where there should have been shadows, by an apple tree,
She saw a hag who laughed to herself and tossed
A golden apple. "Good day, hag," she said.
"Can you tell me how I might find the castle
That lies east of the sun and west of the moon?"
"Whoever comes and calls me hag, haggard
May she sit also, unless it be the lady
Who should marry the prince there. Are you she?
Yes, she says. Yet the way I cannot tell.
Take, rather, this gold apple, mount this horse
To ride to ask my sister, and once there,
Tap him behind the left ear; he will come home."

Long she rode as the patience of stones
And saw again, when it should have been evening,
A hag who played with a golden carding comb.
"If withering were a signature of wisdom,
I were a miracle of sagacity,"
She said, "my brow invisible with laurel,
But I am bare parchment where a word might be,
And any road that might lead to that castle
Is a thing I never knew. All I can offer
By way of blessing is this gold carding comb,
But you might ask my sister; take my own horse.
When he has brought you where she sits, tap him
Behind the left ear; he will come home again."

The third hag said, "I have been young as you,
And shall be so again, unless the stars
Tell lies in the shifty dark, but whether
More pleasure is to be young and pass for fair
Or to be haggard and seem knowledgeable,
I am too wise to choose, and yet the way
That castle lies is a thing I never knew;
But there you will come, late or never. I give you,
Beside that wisdom, this golden spinning wheel,
And if you wish, you may ride my own horse
To ask the East Wind. When you are there,
Tap the beast once behind the left ear,
And he will be off and come to me again."

Oh then she rode such waste of calendars
She should have found the end of weariness
But came instead to the house of the East Wind.
"Oh Wind," she called, "which way would you blow,
Which way might I follow to come to the castle
That lies east of the sun and west of the moon?"
"I, bold of wing beyond the glimpse of morning,
Have found the dark where no birds sleep,
Have shivered and returned, have many times
Heard of that castle, but never blown so far
Nor learned the way. But I have a brother," he said,
"An infinite voyager: be pleased to sit
Between my shoulders and I shall take you there."

Though faster then than summoned ghosts they flew,
Long was that journey as the wisdom of owls
Before they came to the roof of the West Wind.
"For all I am prodigious of voyages,
Whistle heyday and holiday, make light
Of the poor limbs of summer and have sailed
Beyond the hueless sighing of drowned days
Into the dark where no shades sigh,
Have shuddered and come home a different way,
Unholy be the whisper of my name
If ever I were a wind about that tower
Or knew the way; but come with me," he said:
"I have a brother who has blown further than I."

"I might shriek till the world was small
As a turtle's egg; I have whipped my savagery
A pride of days beyond where the world ends
In burning, into the dark where no flames twitch,
Have blessed myself and hastily blown elsewhere,
But never glimpsed wrack nor wisp of that castle,
And whether there be any such place at all
I gravely doubt; but I have a brother
Wields the gale that flaps the chittering dead
Beyond where the world ends in ice; be sure
Unless his storm can shiver your conundrum
It is a thing unknown." The South Wind's wings
Howled, till they came to the door of the North Wind.

"Oh once," he roared, "I blew an aspen leaf
Beyond the glimmering world, over
The glass eaves of time, into that dark
Where no ice gleams; there, bristling, found that other
Wind of fear, but a rage stayed me until
The star-lashed sea, until I found the castle
That lies east of the sun and west of the moon.
But never I told a soul, for there I lay
Three weeks, frail as the aspen leaf, on the wild
Shore before I dared blow home again.
But if you be the lady that you claim,
Stay while I rest tonight and I shall try
Tomorrow if I can fly so far again."

Who has outflown the nightmare? Yet fast
Almost as she they flew in the morning
Beyond all boreal flickerings, headlong
Over the glass eaves of time and found
The breathless dark where no souls stir,
But hair in another wind; broke, almost blind,
At last over a mad famished sea;
Then long as unspoken love they whirled.
But he wearied. The waves snapped at his knees,
The dog-toothed waves, till he whispered, "My wings fail,"
Sinking. But she cried, "I see a white shore,
A shadowy pinnacle that may be the castle
That lies east of the sun and west of the moon."

What if the breakers gulped and craved his thighs?
Where he had set her on the white shore
He fell forward and slept. Already
A foot beyond the frustrate sea there drowsed
Silence of forests, indolent, rimmed
With flutter of birches like birds in the tender
Sun, with thirsty osiers, pale hawthorn,
Perpetual apple trees, the capricious-limbed.
She saw in that light how the castle vanished
Above fancy among faithful clouds,
Saw the door, but nowhere near the door she went,
But sat under a guelder-rose and sang
"Ah, well-a-day," and played with the gold apple.

Till from an upper window of the castle
A princess with a nose three ells long
Called, "Who are you, singing 'well-a-day'
Under my window; and oh what will you take
And give me that golden apple?" "I am a lady
Of foreign ways singing to my own hair
A dirge for diminishing, under a pale tree,
Am a hazard waif blown from the scapegrace sea,
Am an aspen leaf; but nothing you own
Will I exchange for this gold apple,
Unless it should be that I might sleep tonight
Alone all night in his room with the prince
Who lives in this castle." And that could be arranged.

But she was returned, for earnest of gold,
Only a sleeping body and a sleep:
When she was led at evening into his room
Already he lay sleeping; for all she cried
His name aloud, for all she cried and kissed
His face and forehead, all night he lay sleeping.
What might she be but chorus to a dream,
But one who strokes a dream of chrysolite,
Glass pheasants, ducks ridiculous in stone,
A gold salmon in a beryl pool,
As reliquary, as meager communicance
Till daylight, then departs and sits again
By the tower and plays with the gold carding comb?

"Nothing whatever will I take," she said
When the princess called, "for my gold carding comb,
But to sleep tonight by the same prince."
But where was the unrecking fantasy,
The concord of distraught belief
She had named for love and understood by love,
If when she lay, and the second time, beside him
Nothing would answer to her kiss but sleep?
Must she before she wake still find a dream
Wherein she lay beside him, and he, waking,
Dreamed still of her? Although beside him, dream
Of yet more fortunate wakenings; till daylight;
Then sing by a gold spinning wheel, dreaming?

"I am a thirsty lady wishing I walked
Beside no water but a pool of beryl;
I sing to drown the silence of far flowers
And though I am deaf to all sounds other
Than a deafening heart in a distant room, I dream
I wander with my hands over my ears."
She argued with the princess as yesterday,
Parted with the gold spinning wheel. Oh must
Love's many mansions, the patient honeycomb
Of hope unlearn their heavens and at a sleep
Triply be consigned to cerements,
Or must salvation shrink to the unlikely
Monstrance of another's wakening?

Suppose the requisite vigil. Say one lay
Two nights awake beside the prince's room,
Heard crying there, as toward a vanishing spectre,
Told the prince, and he, thus wise against potions
The third night, sleepless, with wide arms received her,
Calling, "Oh love, is blessedness a risk
So delicate in time, that it should be
Tonight you find me? Tomorrow, always tomorrow
It is that my stepmother was to prevail,
It is that I was to marry that other princess.
But we are the sense of dawn beneath pretence
Of an order of darkness. Now lie in wisdom, mindful
Only of love, and leave to me tomorrow."

In the morning, to proud stepdame and coy princess,
"Call me a wry intransigent, a glass
Of fickle weathers, but what care I," he said,
"For decorum, though it be my wedding day?
Shall I be yoked to an unproven woman?
But who she may be can wash this shirt of mine,
Stained with three drops of tallow, white again
As once it was, she and no other lady
Will I marry. All wet the hands who wish;
All beat the board; all wring the linen; all wash
In the one water." Howsoever the princess
Dipped and wrung, the stains ran gray; or stepdame
Scrubbed, the shirt grew black as knavery.

"There is a girl outside the castle door,"
One said who loitered there and watched; "perhaps
She if she tried might wash it white again."
But vexed stepdame and angry princess
Raged then and screamed, "No no! Shall we have a tattered
Waif with outlandish ways for rival, and we
With our royal hands in water?" Yet the prince
Answered, "Let her come in, whoever she be."
She dipped the linen and once drew it forth
White as a leper; drew it forth again
White as blown snow; a third time raised it
Spotless, white as the violent moon; she said,
"How should I not, since all pallor is mine?"

The moon was musing in her high chamber
Among nine thousand mirrors. "Oh what am I,"
She cried, "but a trick of light, and tropically?
I walk in a wild charactry of night,
In a game of darkness figurative with tapers,
Toying with apples, and come upon myself
More often than is meet for sanity.
Oh, who would be shown, save in analogy,
—What for gold handsels and marvelous equerry—
As three hags sitting under an apple tree?
But I walk multifarious among
My baubles and horses; unless I go in a mask
How shall I know myself among my faces?"

"All metaphor," she said, "is magic. Let
Me be diverted in a turning lantern,
Let me in that variety be real.
But let the story be an improvisation
Continually, and through all repetition
Differ a little from itself, as though
Mistaken; and I a lady with foreign ways
To sing therein to my own hair." To the sun,
"You who tomorrow are my Pentecost,
Come dance with me—oh but be white, be wintry;
Oh lest I fall an utter prey to mirrors,
Be a white bear," she said "and come a-walking,
And ask my hand. I am a peasant's daughter."

Is it for nothing that a troupe of days
Makes repeated and perpetual rummage
In the lavish vestry; or should sun and moon,
Finding mortality too mysterious,
Naked and with no guise but its own,
—Unless one of immortal gesture come
And by a mask should show it probable—
Believe a man, but not believe his story?
Say the year is the year of the phoenix.
Now, even now, over the rock hill
The tropical, the lucid moon, turning
Her mortal guises in the eye of a man,
Creates the image in which the world is.

I do not understand the world, father.
By the millpond at the end of the garden
There is a man who slouches listening
To the wheel revolving in the stream, only
There is no wheel there to revolve.

He sits in the end of March, but he sits also
In the end of the garden; his hands are in
His pockets. It is not expectation
On which he is intent, nor yesterday
To which he listens. It is a wheel turning.

When I speak, father, it is the world
That I must mention. He does not move
His feet nor so much as raise his head
For fear he should disturb the sound he hears
Like a pain without a cry, where he listens.

I do not think I am fond, father,
Of the way in which always before he listens
He prepares himself by listening. It is
Unequal, father, like the reason
For which the wheel turns, though there is no wheel.

I speak of him, father, because he is
There with his hands in his pockets, in the end
Of the garden listening to the turning
Wheel that is not there, but it is the world,
Father, that I do not understand.

PROTEUS

By the splashed cave I found him. Not
(As I had expected) patently delusive
In a shape sea-monstrous, terrible though sleeping,
To scare all comers, nor as that bronze-thewed
Old king of Pharos with staring locks,
But under a gray rock, resting his eyes
From futurity, from the blinding crystal
Of that morning sea, his face flicked with a wisp
Of senile beard, a frail somnolent old man.

Who would harness the sea-beast
To the extravagant burden of his question
Must find him thus dreaming of his daughters,
Of porpoises and horses; then pitiless
Of an old man's complaints, unawed
At what fierce beasts are roused under his grasp,
Between the brutal ignorance of his hands
Must seize and hold him till the beast stands again
Manlike but docile, the neck bowed to answer.

I had heard in seven wise cities
Of the last shape of his wisdom: when he,
Giver of winds, father as some said
Of the triple nightmare, from the mouth of a man
Would loose the much-whistled wind of prophecy.
The nothing into which a man leans forward
Is mother of all restiveness, drawing
The body prone to falling into no
Repose at last but the repose of falling.

Wherefore I had brought foot to his island
In the dead of dawn, had picked my way
Among the creaking cypresses, the anonymous
Granite sepulchres; wherefore, beyond these,
I seized him now by sleeping throat and heel.
What were my life, unless I might be stone
To grasp him like the grave, though wisdom change
From supposition to savage supposition;
Unless the rigor of mortal hands seemed deathly?

I was a sepulchre to his pleadings,
Stone to his arguments, to his threats;
When he leapt in a bull's rage
By horn and tail I held him; I became
A mad bull's shadow, and would not leave him;
As a battling ram he rose in my hands;
My arms were locked horns that would not leave his horns;
I was the cleft stick and the claws of birds
When he was a serpent between my fingers.

Wild as heaven erupting into a child
He burst under my fists into a lion;
By mane and foot I grappled him;
Closer to him than his own strength I strained
And held him longer. The sun had fought
Almost to noon when I felt the beast's sinews
Fail, the beast's bristles fall smooth
Again to the skin of a man. I loosed him then.
The head he turned toward me wore a face of mine.

Here was no wisdom but my own silence
Echoed as from a mirror; no marine
Oracular stare but my own eyes
Blinded and drowned in their reflections;
No voice came but a voice we shared, saying,
"You prevail always, but, deathly, I am with you
Always." I am he, by grace of no wisdom,
Who to no end battles the foolish shapes
Of his own death by the insatiate sea.

Countenance like lightning, why do you stand
In ebony raiment after no invocation
Suddenly where I knew no face, as though
You had stood so forever?

                  —Say that the light
That is today, after so long becomes me,
Or that love's pleading incense that rose once
For mercy pleads now no longer, whereupon
The air conceives new clarity, and there
Suddenly I am visible. But know
I was the urgency that framed that love
And made it cry for mercy, the question
And the voice of the woman whispering, "Be content,
Be content."

             I am that which you lost
Behind you which you seek before you, for I
Am certain: sullen under your gaiety
And still its root and entrepreneur; footloose,
Not musical, but moving in all your music,
Assumed in all apostrophes.

                 Think of me
As of a dusk through which no herds go home,
Quiet, perhaps, yet inexcusably
Disquieting, with a voice of infinite patience,
Gentle until resisted, like sheep bells
In the next valley.

And I am he
With whom on a desperate hill, because I was
The closest combatant, always last night
You wrestled, as with the angel of your dark,
And overcame, yet in defeat who found
Such re-creation, always I rose with dawn
Enlarged by falling, as though I were the angel,
Equally, of your day. Yet one day
—Heaven and hills having endured—your arm,
Hopeless long since of conquest, will strike upon
Fatal surprise and end me there; and through
The evening slanting always at hand among
Unstartled trees, under a world of birds
Settling like dust despite the clang of triumph,
It will be your body that will fall.

DECEMBER: OF APHRODITE

Whatever the books may say, or the plausible
Chroniclers intimate: that I was mad,
That an unsettling wind that season
Fretted my sign and fetched up violence
From the vagaries of dream, or even that pride
Is a broad road with few turnings, do not
Believe them. In her name I acted.

(Vidal once, the extravagant of heart,
For the love of a woman went mad, mad as a dog,
And the wolves ate him; Hercules, crazed
By that jealous goddess, murdered his children;
Samson, from a woman's lap, woke blinded,
Turning a mill in Gaza; Adam, our father,
Eating from his wife's hand, fell from the garden.)

Not that from heaven she twisted my tenderness
Into a hand of rage, nor because she delighted
In burnt offering, I in my five senses
Cut throats of friends, burned the white harvest, waged
Seven months' havoc even among
Her temples; but because she waited always
There in the elegant shell, asking for sweetness.

And though it was in her name the land was ravaged,
Spilled and dishonored, let it not be said
That by her wiles it was done, nor that she gave
That carnage her blessing. All arrogant demons
Pretending changelessness, who came first when she called,
Have faded and are spent, till out of the strong,
Without death, she conjured the honeycomb.

She sits at evening under a gray arch
Where many marvels fell, where all has fallen:
The blue over her dolphins, the poplar leaves,
The cold rain, all but the grave myrtle
And the rings of her ringdoves. The doge of one calendar
Would give her a name of winter, but where I stand
In the hazed gold of her eyes, the world is green.

Was there truly in that afternoon
No sorcery, when the leaves between us
In the October garden fell like words
Through the long sun before the gathering winter;
Was there no enchantment but your imputation?
I was a name inconstant; I had come,
Unlooked for, from the shifting sea, my face
A field for doubting, my tales untrustworthy;
You believed, and therewith I was credible.

And that stern evening, speaking of snares
Where the hunter had fallen, where even the wise might fall,
Or speaking, in November, of primroses,
When doubt possessed me, and my eyes fell
To stones, half trusting in stones, and my mind fell
To a merciless winter of bleak words, yet you
Beyond words believed me to be a gentle
Season, and I, as from sleep returning,
Was thence the sign and green wind of spring.

You are the tender hazel and diviner
Whose faith is delicacy; yet had you
Believed me anything but what I was
I should have come—still without violence
But gently as that legendary beast
The unicorn, who did not exist
Until conceived in the mind of a virgin—
Through the woods of change, and laid down my head
To fill the lap and hand of your supposition.

For you, by all the faiths in which we figure,
Are undeceivable: we are not ourselves
And I but a shadow in your superstition
Unless love be an imagination
Framing the singular metaphor of coherence
In the dying riot of random generation,
Unless it be the passion of an order
Informs you so to this innocent
Authority, this peculiar knowledge.

And have you not become, by much believing,
Yourself the prime breath, the infusion of the real
Upon this dust? I walked incredible
As death, a gaunt preposterous ghost, until
Your creed included me among the living:
But not until I had, as from despair,
Abandoned claim to all the probable senses
And had become your trope and tenet merely,
Could I inherit the familiar body.

I am renewed as you imagine me
For all the orders which love believes
Are the one order. There, listening, the child
In love with wonder, ascribing contradictions
To the different gesture of an heroic world,
Attributing the bruited failure
To an alien but more excellent mode
Of triumph, creates a possible
World for the impossible legionary.

There forlorn clown and painted masquer
Do not move in a demonstration merely,
Cynical, of the necessity of error,
But perform an ordered rage of jubilation,
And the eye in love with compassion believes
The figures of compassion: the mad girl
Mourning her father, the fretted prince delaying
Particular confusion till the confusion
Of death be absolute and general.

The idiom of order is celebration,
An elegance to redeem the graceless years;
So those the nine-years-enraged for a filched doxy
Who contend forever in the fanciful song
Are the real, and those who with tangible
Bronze fought are now the unbelievable dead,
Their speech inconceivable, their voyages in vain,
Their deeds inaccurate, save as they coincide
With the final tale, the saving celebration.

But you, believing, name a new paradigm
That existed, nonetheless, before
The hour of your believing: for the order
Is, although the place where it exist
Be nowhere but a possibility;
And your believing spins continually
Its own newness: as time continues
Out of the possibility of itself.
Time is a creature like the unicorn.

It is by your faith that I believe, I am.
Therein is genesis, as though a man,
In love with existence, should bring to belief
A divinity, an imagination
That might move upon the idea of nothing
And imagine a man; as though a man could make
A mirror out of his own divinity,
Wherein he might believe himself, and be.
So, in your articles, we love, you are.

And our hands are a shape of confidence,
A gesture of releasing, where joy is always
Young as its own beginning. Thus the falling
Water is confident and falls, thus summer
Confidently fails, and both are new
As often as they fall. Believing is
Conception, is without artifice the making
Perpetually new, is that first holy
Aura and ordinance of creation.

I have pronounced you the single luminary,
And we are housed in an embrace of whiteness,
But shadows would threaten and the dark descend
In all the rooms where we believe. Oh love,
Believe this candor indivisible,
That I, perfected in your love, may be,
Against all dissolution sovereign,
Endlessly your litany and mirror,
About your neck the amulet and song.

CANSO

Must there be in the continuum and whorl
Of love always this whisper, on the tender
Horizon this supposition always,
A boreal shudder of feared light, a voice
That in my own voice cries to you, "Love, love,
Must you, in time more compromised than I,
In time be spoken from me, and I be left
To sit alone as it were forever,
Telling over the scandal that is time
In this dark room where the pictures hang
On the silence as though it were a wall?"

Or why should it be that we walk always
Slowly as though to lag long after time
And be alone there, that we perform
All of affection with a ceremony
Of more than patience, as though there were to be
Presently an end, or that I see you
Always, my eyes clear as on that day
When in fear of winter we watched the high ridge,
The tilted plain complacent in such summer,
Knowing we saw them for the last time, and love
Became itself a sense of leave-taking?

If you, if you my word and so my life
And so the mode and vessel of my death,
Should die before me, I would not go
—Although turned phantom by your truancy—
Calling the earth of you; neither, impelled
By what pain soever, with a zeal
As of an antiquarian, cull, compose
At last a vacancy of you and there become
An impresario of emptiness
Swaying before defection. What are the patterned
Potsherds to him who knows what wine there was?

It is not the comforts of a chiliast,
Nor of a mind mnemonic and apart
As an old man rocking in his doorway at
Irrelevant evening that I would wish to hear
Mumbling, "There was a world, there was, as it were,
A world wherein she walked once and was loved.
Is this, among worlds, not similar? And if
A tree wherein a throstle sang should lose
Not leaves but the bird only, would it not
Be, though without that singing, yet as green
As ever?" It would be the tree had died.

And what profit would there be to me then
In the lure of song, the twanged incantation,
Which on a time so played on savagery
With order, that the beasts came: phoenix and sow,
Cat, unicorn, chimaera came, swimming
Through the incredibility of themselves

As through the air, to sit in a round,
To hear, to hear a wish? Unless they might
By virtue of the same order, as by love,
But changelessly, stand listening so forever
And there be real in the ultimate song.

Unless you also in that animal
Constraint of death having become
Incredible, might nevertheless by such
Enchantment, as once by love, but changelessly,
Be tamed out of that emptiness, and come
To stand again, as in flesh, in a place
Of possibility. Unless there be
Within the figure of mortality
This mind of heaven whereby I may
Fashion the lips and be as breath again
In the mouth in which you were a word.

Or may the mind of heaven be a mind
Of questions? As: is there not a country
Or the negation of a country, where
The mortal tree where the bird sang, the season
Where you walked living, once existed only
In their own deaths before their tides and branches
Were from negation made? It is that world
That I would have wherein you might be loved,
And I would seek it in its own death, and shape
Its life out of your death, for it must be
Created out of the nothing that you are.

There must be found, then, the imagination
Before the names of things, the dicta for
The only poem, and among all dictions
That ceremony whereby you may be named
Perpetual out of the anonymity
Of death. I will make out of my grief
A river, and my rage shall be the coin
To catch its ferryman; out of my fear
A dog shall spring; I will fling my bitterness
To stop his throats. I will myself become
A Hades into which I can descend.

It will be a domain of déjà-vus,
The final most outlandish fastness of
Familiarity without memory,
Whose set dimensions, whose mode of privacy
And mode of pain I with my living breath
Shall enter, saying, "Like an Icarus
I have fallen into my shadow." There shall be seen
The death of the body walking in shapes of bodies,
Departure's self hid in a guise of sojourn,
As it seems among the living. But on those hills
The shadows of sheep are folded, not the sheep.

But on those lakes or the mirages of
Those lakes not birds are reflected, but the flight
Of birds across no sky. It is nevertheless
A place of recognition, though it be
Of recognition of nothing; a place of knowledge
Though it be knowledge of nothing; in this land

No landscape but a demeanor of distance
Where interchangeably the poles are death
And death, as in an opposition of mirrors
Where no beginning is, no end, I have lived
Not recognizing, for as long as knowledge.

Say it is the idea of a place
That has no imagination of its own;
Yet in these nothing-fertile notions of
Valleys, this static nature in a mind
Of motion were all motion and all mind
And the actual lake moving its metaphor
Under real birds conceived, although conceived
Only for uses elsewhere. It is between
These twin antinomies that I must walk
Casting, it seems, no image; between these poles
Of vanity that I must make you real.

And say that even here, this place that I
Make in a shadow, though I cast no image,
Make even as I walk here, there must be
In a kingdom of mirrors a king among
Mirrors, although he be no more
Than that image I do not cast: as it were
An ear upon the infinite silence, a something
Sovereign, before whom in some manner
I can stand to dispute his sovereignty
As before a mirror, saying, "Master of these
Echoing revels whose silence I violate . . ."

Or better, to a genius more alien there,
A deeper shadow more sorrowfully reposed,
Folded almost in memory, but sconced
In the necessity of that kingdom
As in an ancient throne, Persephone,
To say, "Oh Moon among such sanity,
Oh Other among the simulacra, Virgin
Madonna of the lap of sleep, conceiving
All flesh and holiness, I come to you calling,
Making you in a prayer, that your name
May know my voice and conceive a mercy."

Take it for answer when the hair lifts
There in no wind as in an insolence
Of wind: it is the self of highness in
That hollow, counterpart and partisan
Born of the argument, who listens. "Mistress,
I speak what you know: where the shadows were real
I loved a lady. Be not surprised
Now if I stand beyond lamentations, fictive
In places prepared for loss: save where she is
I am anomaly. Oh Name, what is her name
In anonymity, that I may call

And she be with me? For what is your Lord
Of Anonymity, Lord of Nothing
And Nowhere, if I know his name?
Unless he be also furtively somewhere
A lord of names? Mistress, what is your
Arrogant Chief Jack of Death but a hollow

Tale, my figment, nothing at all, unless
He be somewhere alive, alive? Tell him
That I who cast no shadow taunt him there
With the bogey of his name. How would he be
Death if I should imagine him otherwise?

Or rather, let me not be told her name
In death, for with such appellation
If I should call it would be in the attributes
Of death that she would come, and I am not used
To such reserves between us. But now, should I
Pronounce her as though she were alive,
Say it is a new word I make: not new
Merely for what the old words would not cover,
But an affirmation of what heretofore
Had not been so; let what has never been,
Suddenly, in terms of what is, be.

For I am instructed of this silence, Lady,
That what is not is of a nature
With what has never been; and Mention, though
It be the scholiast of memory,
Makes yet its presences from emptiness,
Speaks for the first time always, an improvisation,
Though in an ancient mode, a paradigm
For the unmentionable. Yet may the word
Be celebration of a permanence,
Make, so, a presence and a permanence,
The articulate dance, the turning festival."

"Creation," she says, "is your idea, then?"
"Lady, you know. Creation waits upon
The word; but you in silence are the conception
And the consent of speech, the metaphor
In the midst of chaos, whose word is love.
And though I would in her name shatter, drown
The clamorous dialectic of this silence
With irrefutable song, and though I had
Imagination to remove mountains
Out of their shadows, and did not have this love,
I were a vain instrument; I were nothing."

There in her shadow, voice in a gown of silence,
She says, "I, though I be the predicate
Of love, the image in the blather of death
To make that monotone intelligible
To itself, am yet this image in the blather
And terms of death, whose parlance will not be
By its own intelligibility gainsaid.
Creation," she says, "is perforce and always
The creation of a world, the world; it is
An infinite nature making infinite nature,
But death exacts therefor an infinite price.

What if, by uttering the terms of living
Upon this mortuary air, your head
Should become anomalous on your body
And neither be satisfied, but both walk, strange,
Fictive, among real familiars, or
Real but immortal among the figurative

But dying; or, undelighted by what fades,
Alien, unbelieving, unbelieved,
Live in a heart of celebration only?"
"If the terms stand, so be it. There in her
Living intimacy I am not foreign."

"There must be, before creation is,
A concept of beginnings, a notion
As of a rocking cradle not yet rocking
Where yet no cradle is: therein may time
The prodigy impossibly conceived
Upon itself, born of itself and still
Unborn, be laid, the sage, the quiet child
Conceiving timelessness." "I imagine
A song not temporal wherein may walk
The animals of time; I conceive a moment
In which time and that timelessness begin."

Creation is not raw, is not refined.
In a landscape of raw antecedent
Before belief, or a country refined
Beyond belief, without motion, without
Farewells, to which one does not say good-bye,
I, conceiving of creation, have
Conceived the novelty of farewell. I said,
"Let it be a time the sand whereof
May run somewhere besides away, may run
Nowhere perhaps at all. A time that lies
Immutable under eternal leaves."

And I therewith am already elsewhere
In a littoral not time's, though time has been
Godfather there and blessing, an ambit
As though of memory, but not memory's,
Where with a word I divide the literal
From the dead. Why should I notice the waters
Sundering from the waters, or suddenly
The first tree waving ancient fronds, or how
From novel shadows the new beasts come, the savage
Modulations of holiness, in love's name
Where other names are profanation?

For it is you that are the world thereof,
You whom, possessing, I have still desired,
And, touching, have still dreamed of; you the sense,
The echo there waiting upon this word,
The circle making all within it real,
The sole order; for I have painfully
Wrought you from vacancy to this full air
And sung you to the tender instrument
Of my ten fingers till you have become
The poem in whose arbor we may kiss,
The summer into which we can ascend.

You know the story, its dénouement. You know
Death is by definition a terrain
Of no return save to itself, where all
Appearances are voices calling, "Look
Now, oh look if now only"; is a face whereon
To look is to know loss; and what if I

Should turn but once, and you vanish? The song is nothing
If not a resurrection. Therein I sing you,
Love, always more real, though in the fraying
Edges of patience the teased harpies
Hone the incredible silence against their tongues.

CANSO

I believe at dark solstice in the white moon sailing new;
And in my love, and in her hand, though the green shoot
    withered,
And in the twice-joining sea between us, and I believe
I lay long with the cold dead, although the word was summer,
The violent dead, and now
When the sun hangs in the low branches
Bleeding, and phoenix-like the white-feathered
Childish sibyl sings in the leaves of the dead year,
And northerly on another island
She smiles into the swirling mist, her trees
Half-sleeved in white, I believe
Resurrection stirs like the robin
Through the waters of the dead, and the buried blood,
Through the rain of two islands
To float like a lotus into the waking year
And stand wide-eyed like a lamb; I believe the dead
Mirrors of the sea shine soft with her new image always.

She is clear amber and the heaven's face
Seen under simple waters: there below
The lights, the vessels, the shore, the drift-shells stroking
The whipped weeds of the tide-race,
Under the fish flying and the laughter of her dolphins,
First cold, final echoes, and the salt dead, she is marine
And always the child among horses
At autumn by the dove-keep,

And the woman in tears in the green
Drowned wood in no time by the lost house on the slow
River, and always she is ancient as the sea's daughters,
As the green beginning; always the rites of her tides keen
Tender in my ears, her birds call me fair, her twining hands
Run gentle to my hands for honey, her lips bid me love
Her limbs in coral and the bursts of her dolphins
Always, the softness of her sea-changes
And the pride of her horses.

And there where the spume flies and the mews echoed and
    beckoned
The bowing drowned, because in her hands love and the one
    song
Leap and the long faith is born gladly, there through the
    waters
Of the dead, like the robin, singing, like the floating year,
The deep world in one island,
Streaming white from every dark-folded
Valley, till the green burgeons, and the long
Ghosts dripping leave the washed gold and the mounding joy,
The fruit swaying yellow, the shimmering birches
And the wise beaches lapped with the serpents and dead
Of the forgiving waters,
There, across green the gold light hanging,
The bees in the rosemary, the flashing pigeons,
Bud and harvest together,
The world in one island, because her hands are joy,
To no trumpet, all tongues singing the full silence,
Rises now and forever to gleam new as the white sea.

(Who sings now of the desperate seas, the bleak
Voyages by darkness, when the wind fell,
When the shadow waxed between us, and hails faded
And oar-sounds, when the last streak
Of the other lantern dwindled, and groped wakes, one by one
Ended in nothing, when separately we sailed seeking
By the four points and the foreign stars
Falling that may guide no man,
The treasure, the landfall, the morning,
Gray ease after night-fear, after shoal and cold swell
The harbor of one hand? Who sings, after the black whale-beds,
Tideless, and nautilus-marches, of the poles, the towers
Where we came each alone, of the widdershin wheels turning
By blue flames, where we lay dead in the grave's waters,
    though all
The world was summer? For the seven seas are one,
The four winds, and all journey and treasures
And islands, and the sung stars.)

Here is the gate of psalms, swordless, and the angel's country
For which we became as children; known earth and known
    heaven
Washed new in the ancient wonder; here in the high pastures,
Its roots in another story, offering innocence
Like apples, is the same tree;
Under the leaves and holy shadows
The same brightness springs where the stones begin
Laughter and green singing in the ancient rivers
And the new hours like the first shallows run;
There beyond pools and sheep bells where the dark browses

Already the gold pastures,
Are hushed grass and the bell of silence,
The silk-gray dusk, the mackerel sky for the moonrise,
Then the same moon riding new
Over the fields, the lulled falling of four rivers
And the praising hills and white leaves of paradise,
And swimming silver across her eyes and in the same sea.

Nightingales will sleep in the sycamores
Till there is no night; here will not the dark
Worm come with his sliding season, though the leaves fall,
Nor the snake in the small hours
Molest the young doves and thrushes with the snare of his
    hands
Nor sicken the drowsing fruit with the shadow of his tongue,
Nor chains nor temptations, till the end
Of time, nor any serpent,
Save the long tides, till the sea return.
She is clear amber, and the dawn found in the dark
By faith at last, by following sea-sounds, by the lost
Shells' singing, and like the sea she walks always beside me
Telling, and the warm deeps of her waters are never sung
Where, amid fathomless musics subtle beneath voices,
Softly she draws me down with her whispers and hands,
Her floods and eyes, face to face, telling me
Her white love, world without end.

Now, now I enter the first garden and the promised moon,
The silver of her thighs and shoulders; oh here where the
    sheaves
And shadows sway to her breath, in the caroling darkness
We embrace at last, and are night and morning together
And the gray-gold afternoon
Of marvels sinking over the hill
And the first and last tree; and all the leaves
Of our deaths are chanting, "Holy, holy, holy
Always were taper-light and ember-light,
Moon-light, the bowing stars, and that first glory still
Singing day from the darkness;
And never, save unto our amen
Shall the white sea surrender its dead, oh never,
Oh never. Amen. Amen."
We listen, and shall here, love, with the sea's holy
Song in the shells of our ears, lie down forever
To sleep in the turning garden for as long as the sea.